The entrance to the 'home pipe' at Boarstall Decoy, Buckinghamshire.

Duck Decoys

Andrew Heaton

A Shire book

Published in 2001 by Shire Publications Ltd,
Cromwell House, Church Street, Princes Risborough,
Buckinghamshire HP27 9AA, UK.
(Website: www.shirebooks.co.uk)

Copyright © 2001 by Andrew Heaton.
First published 2001.
Shire Album 361. ISBN 0 7478 0497 4.
Andrew Heaton is hereby identified as the author of this
work in accordance with Section 77 of the Copyright,
Designs and Patents Act 1988.

British Library Cataloguing in Publication Data:
Heaton, Andrew.
Duck decoys. – (A Shire album; 361)
1. Decoys (Hunting) 2. Fowling
I. Title
639.1'2841
ISBN 0 7478 0497 4

Cover: *A decoyman driving wild ducks down a pipe; 'The Book of Duck Decoys, Their Construction, Management and History', by Ralph Payne-Gallwey, 1886.*

ACKNOWLEDGEMENTS
Illustrations are acknowledged as follows: Abbotsbury Tourism Ltd, pages 28 (top left), 35 (centre right); APS (UK), page 24 (bottom); Crown Copyright/MOD, pages 21 (bottom), 33 (top); Crown Copyright/NMR, page 35 (top left); English Nature, page 36 (bottom); Essex County Council, pages 19, 20 (top); the Field Studies Council, pages 5 (bottom), 32; *The Independent*/Syndication, page 29 (bottom left); the National Trust, pages 8 (bottom), 9 (top), 29 (top left), 34 (middle); Norfolk Wildlife Trust, page 37 (top); Paul Leonard/Thorne and Hatfield Moors Conservation Forum, page 8 (top); *The Times*, page 26 (top); the Wildfowl and Wetlands Trust, pages 11 (bottom), 14 (top), 28 (top right), 29 (top right). Illustrations on pages 4 (both), 5 (top), 7 (both), 12 (left), 13 (bottom left and top right), 17 (top right), 22, 23 (middle), 25 (right), 27 (bottom), 28 (bottom) and 29 (bottom right) are taken from *The Book of Duck Decoys, Their Construction, Management and History* by Ralph Payne-Gallwey (1886) and those on pages 6 (bottom), 13 (top left), 20 (bottom) and 30 from *British Duck Decoys of Today, 1918* by Joseph Whitaker (1918). All the other photographs and drawings are by the author unless an alternative source is stated in the caption.

The assistance of the active decoymen (Jim Worgan, Boarstall; Ivan Newton, Borough Fen; Dave Paynter, Berkeley; Dick Dalley, Abbotsbury) is gratefully acknowledged. Thanks are also due to many others who helped with information, illustrations and site visits, especially John Fullard at Slimbridge and John Norris at Nacton; Frank Barkley of Ashby Decoy Golf Club; Alastair Roach of the National Trust; Elizabeth Whittle of Cadw; Ioan Thomas at Titchmarsh; Martin Limbert, Doncaster Museum; various people from English Heritage, the Field Studies Council, the National Trust, and the Wildlife Trusts; custodians of Sites and Monuments Records; staff at the English Nature library at Peterborough; colleagues at the Environment Agency, Solihull; the Taylor family of Skellingthorpe, where I first became interested in decoys; and my wife, Anne, who read and criticised an early draft.

Printed in Malta by Gutenberg Press Limited, Gudja Road,
Tarxien PLA 19, Malta.

Contents

Mallard fly into a pipe at Berkeley New Decoy, Gloucestershire. (E. E. Jackson/WWT)

Introduction

Duck decoys played a significant part in the rural economy for several centuries as a source of food for country houses and urban markets. Some still remain, enigmatic features of the countryside, interesting both for their history and their natural history.

From at least the thirteenth century, in areas such as the Fens, wild ducks and geese had been caught in large numbers during the period in summer when they moulted their feathers, making them flightless. Nets were staked out in a funnel shape, ending in closed cones, and the grounded wildfowl were driven into them. There are reports of three or four thousand ducks being taken at a single drive. Such mass destruction, involving also young birds incapable of flight, was eventually made illegal in 1710 to protect wildfowl numbers.

In areas such as the Fens, the practice of herding flightless wildfowl during the moulting period into temporary pens was a precursor to the more sophisticated decoys.

4

View along a decoy pipe being worked by a decoyman and dog. This would normally be in the morning or early afternoon.

Diagram of a decoy pipe in use. As the dog runs around the reed screens, the curious ducks follow it, moving ever further down the pipe.

The idea of permanent structures as devices for trapping wildfowl originated in Holland, probably in the sixteenth century. These structures were known in Dutch as *eendekooi*, from *eenden*, meaning ducks, and *kooi*, a cage. This was contracted in English to *decoy*, the word later taking on the broader meaning of 'to lure'.

A decoy, as developed in Holland, essentially consisted of a central pond, from which radiated a number of arms covered with netting, in which the birds were trapped. Which decoy was the first to be constructed in England is uncertain, but it appears to be one at Waxham in Norfolk. This was built around 1620 by Sir William Woodhouse, who is recognised as the first person to introduce properly planned decoys into East Anglia.

Amongst early decoys the best documented is certainly that completed at St James's Park, London, in 1665 for King Charles II. A Dutchman, Sydrach Hilcus, was brought over from Holland, at a cost of £30, to construct the decoy. The accounts and details of materials used are still in existence. The decoy was worked by the Royal Decoyman,

5

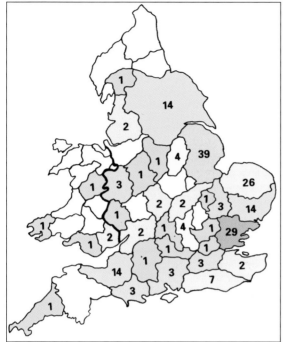

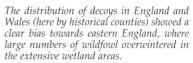

The distribution of decoys in England and Wales (here by historical counties) showed a clear bias towards eastern England, where large numbers of wildfowl overwintered in the extensive wetland areas.

an Englishman named Edward Storey (whose house stood at Storey's Gate).

Given the links between Holland and Lincolnshire, it is not surprising that south Lincolnshire, together with Essex, was the first stronghold of decoy construction. As the success of decoys became apparent, they spread across England, especially in the extensive wetland areas of East Anglia and Somerset. The heyday of the decoys was from the early eighteenth to the mid nineteenth century, when wildfowl were caught in huge numbers.

Much of our knowledge of duck decoys comes from Sir Ralph Payne-Gallwey's comprehensive *The Book of Duck Decoys, Their Construction, Management and History*, published in 1886. Payne-Gallwey realised that the use of decoys was a dying art and decided to document all he could of the decoys of the British Isles, their structures and methods of working, at a time when remains and memories of decoys that have now vanished were still available.

Despite gaps in Payne-Gallwey's knowledge, he managed to list a total of 215 decoys, 188 in England, together with five in Wales and twenty-two in Ireland. (There has apparently never been a working decoy in Scotland – one was begun near Findhorn Bay but was never completed.) At the time he was writing, only forty-four decoys were still working, the majority having already fallen into disuse.

The last decoy constructed in Britain may have been that built by Payne-Gallwey himself in 1885 at his Thirkleby Park estate near Thirsk in North Yorkshire. By this time the age of the decoys was largely over, and a steady decline in their use followed.

A portrait of Sir Ralph Payne-Gallwey.

The structure of a duck decoy

Designs of duck decoys varied, depending upon the site. Some were built on to the edges of large lakes, others were adaptations of existing ponds, whilst the majority were newly constructed. All of them consisted of a central area of open water on which the ducks would land, and a number of netted arms (or 'pipes') leading off it into which the birds would be enticed and trapped. Pipes generally numbered from three to eight (though greater and lesser numbers were known) and extended from the central pond in different directions, so as to be useful under different wind conditions.

The purpose-built decoys were constructed around a central pond usually of 1–2 acres (0.4–0.8 hectares), and rarely more than 4 acres (1.6 ha), in extent; Payne-Gallwey thought $1^{1}/_{4}$ acres (0.5 ha), excluding the pipes, to be the optimum size. The pond would have a uniform depth of 2–3 feet (0.6–0.9 metres), shelving towards the edges. Around the edges would be 'landings', flat short-grass areas where the birds could rest.

Exceptions to this preferred size were seen in the decoys on large lakes. Here, decoy pipes were attached to the edges of the lake, usually grouped at one end or around a sheltered bay. These decoys often proved less effective – the birds were too far out to be enticed into a pipe, and the deeper water tended to attract diving ducks, which were more difficult to trap.

The pipes consisted of curving ditches, 60–70 yards (55–64 metres) long, which tapered as they led away from the pond: at the pond edge, the pipe width would be 18–21 feet (5.5–6.4 metres), gradually narrowing to 2 feet (0.6 metres) at the further end.

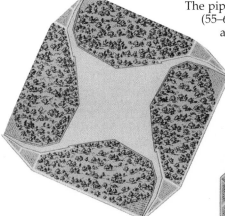

Above: *A plan of a typical four-pipe decoy, such as that at Coombe Abbey, Warwickshire.*

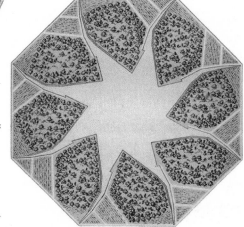

Right: *Payne-Gallwey's plan of an eight-pipe decoy, based on that at Lakenheath, Suffolk.*

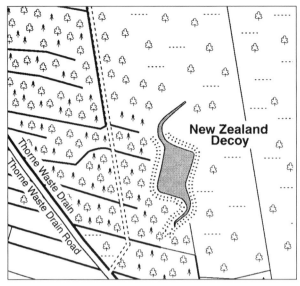

New Zealand decoy, on the peatlands of Thorne Moors, South Yorkshire – an unusual two-pipe structure. (From Limbert, 1998)

The net structure was supported by a series of hoops straddling each pipe, set at intervals of 5 feet (1.5 metres). The most durable hoops were made of round iron, though wooden poles were also used (of willow, ash or wych elm). Typically, the first hoop, at the pond edge and hence with a spread of 21 feet (6.4 metres), would stand 15 feet (4.5 metres) high above the water surface. At the second

Restoring the 'home pipe' at Boarstall Decoy, Buckinghamshire, in 1986 – erecting the main hoops.

bend of the pipe (which was not regularly curved) the hoop was 10 feet (3 metres) wide and 9 feet (2.7 metres) high. The last hoop cleared the water surface by only 2 feet (0.6 metres).

Over the hoops was stretched the net of diamond mesh. Sisal or hemp netting was used; wire mesh was not favoured, as it whistles in the wind and can damage the birds. Beyond the fixed net, at the narrow end of the pipe, came the detachable tunnel net – the device in which the birds were caught. With a length of around 15 feet (4.5 metres), the tunnel net had a head hoop, a ring 2 feet (0.6 metres) in diameter, which slid into slotted upright posts situated at the end of the fixed pipe.

Along the length of each pipe ran a series of about eleven screens, constructed of post and rail frames with a covering of reeds and peep-holes for the decoyman. The first screen was 28 feet (8.5 metres) long, the others 12 feet (3.6 metres). The surrounding screens stopped at the second bend of the pipe. The positioning of the screens allowed some overlap; low fences ran between each adjacent pair, as dog leaps, the first of these being known as the 'yackoop' – a corruption of 'wake up'.

A section of a pipe, with the net stretched over metal hoops, at Boarstall Decoy. Traditionally, nets would be tarred to preserve them.

The narrow end of the 'home pipe' at Boarstall, Buckinghamshire, coming out of the wood into open ground. At Oakley Park, Shropshire, pipes were known as 'flues'.

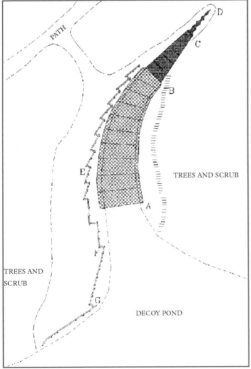

All around the decoy pond, woodland was planted to provide a barrier against disturbance – for effective catching it was essential that the ducks were not disturbed prematurely. However, the end of the pipes was left open and unshaded so that the birds could see the sky and would regard it as a safe area into which to fly.

Decoying is essentially a winter activity (generally from October to March). The reason for having several pipes to a decoy is that one will be more effective depending on the wind direction. Ducks much prefer to take off into the wind; if the wind was blowing directly into a pipe mouth, they would turn around and escape. The wind is also used to carry human scent away from the pond. A smouldering piece of peat was sometimes used to disguise the smell of the decoyman.

The layout of a decoy pipe: AB, net fixed to hoops; BC, net fixed to hoops and side boards; CD, tunnel net; E, reed screens; F, head show place; G, yackoop.

10

Above: *The reed screens alongside one of the pipes at Borough Fen Decoy, near Peterborough, showing the way they overlap, with dog leaps between.*

At Nacton (Orwell Park), Suffolk, Tom Baker prepares to remove birds from the tunnel net, the detachable section at the end of the pipe.

Working the decoy

The principle of trapping is that ducks are encouraged to enter a pipe and swim up until they reach a point where their retreat to the safety of the pond can be cut off and they can be driven into the tunnel net. One method of achieving this relies upon the natural instinct of wildfowl to react to a potential predator.

Ducks on open water will respond to the appearance of a predator on the water's edge by swimming towards it, but remaining a safe distance out. If the predator moves along the edge, the ducks will follow it, all the time remaining the same safe distance away – keeping an eye on potential danger whilst not taking too much risk. This is most readily seen in relation to foxes but is effective with other possible predators, not least dogs. The behaviour has been made use of in the practice of 'dogging' a decoy – training a dog to attract birds into a pipe.

When the decoyman was sure that ducks were present in an appropriate position close to a pipe entrance (encouraged by feeding), he would send his dog to jump over the yackoop, run along the first screen, and then disappear behind it; this would be repeated one or two times. The sudden appearance and disappearance of the dog would attract the curiosity of the ducks, which would swim towards it to investigate. The decoyman, out of sight behind the screens, would then move quietly forwards, sending the dog to jump over the dog leap and run around the next screen. This would be repeated screen by screen along the pipe, drawing the birds down under the net.

Once the ducks had reached a sufficient distance down the pipe, the decoyman would return to the 'head show place' at the entrance

Left: *A decoyman driving the lured ducks up the pipe towards the tunnel end. The tunnel net is hidden by the curve of the pipe.*

Below: *Ducks respond to the appearance of a dog in the pipe at Berkeley New Decoy, Gloucestershire. (J. B. Blossom/WWT)*

Above left: *'Peeping through the spyhole', an illustration by A. H. Patterson from Whitaker (1918). A wooden peg was inserted through the reeds and twisted to create a small viewing hole.*

Above right: *The view down a pipe from the 'head show place', where the decoyman would show himself and push the birds down towards the tunnel net.*

and reveal himself to the ducks in the pipe, whilst remaining hidden from those on the pond. This would then drive the birds down the pipe, into the tunnel net; they would be unable to detect that the end was closed because of the curve of the pipe. Trapped in the tunnel net, the ducks could then be killed and extracted by the decoyman. This was accomplished, according to Payne-Gallwey, by 'breaking the necks of the captured fowl artistically'.

Left: *A decoyman taking birds from the tunnel net (also known as the purse or trammel-net).*

Below: *Don, a Kooikerhondje which was formerly used to work the decoy at Boarstall, Buckinghamshire. The breed name means 'cage dog'.*

The piper hurdles a dog leap at Borough Fen Decoy, Cambridgeshire. Many different breeds of dogs have been used as pipers. At Hornby Castle, Yorkshire, the piper was dressed in a foxskin coat and brush.

A dog trained and used in working a decoy in this manner needs to be extremely obedient, able to respond to silent commands and carry out its duties without taking notice of the encroaching wildfowl. The dogs were traditionally given the name of Piper. Such dogs tended to be fox-like in form, small with a bushy tail and a reddish colouration. A Dutch breed, the Kooikerhondje, was specially developed to work in decoys. In England, various types of dogs have been used as pipers, including terriers, Labradors, mongrels, even a Newfoundland. Payne-Gallwey experimented with the use of a cat, a ferret and a rabbit (each effective but impossible to train) and tried using a monkey, which attracted

John Norris, who maintains Nacton Decoy, Suffolk, with two Duck-tollers. Originally bred in Canada for shooting purposes, they are now beginning to be used as decoy dogs.

14

the ducks at first but then scared them away when it turned towards them! A stuffed fox (or stoat) on a long pole has worked successfully.

An alternative approach to dogging was feeding. A certain number of tame ducks would be kept on the decoy to attract the wild ducks, which might otherwise be wary of a totally empty pond. Payne-Gallwey suggested twenty to thirty of these 'call ducks'. A little grain, hempseed or potatoes would be fed on to the pond during the day, the amount being critical: too little, and the tame birds tended to rush up the pipes for more, deterring the wild ones; too much, and all the birds stayed on the pond, out of the pipes.

When sufficient wild ducks had been attracted in, the decoyman, hidden by the screens, would walk away from the pond towards the pipe end, throwing grain over the top of each screen. As with dogging, at the point where the retreat of the birds could be barred, he would reveal himself and drive them into the tunnel end. (An early custom was for a decoyman to wear a scarlet coat, thought to be more frightening to ducks.) When killing the quarry, tame birds would be recognised and spared, either by their colouration (often white) or because they had been marked by a notch cut in the webbing of one foot. The tame birds would be given their main food in late evening when the wild birds had left.

Feeding was found to be more effective than dogging at coastal decoys, especially if intertidal areas were covered for long periods by high tides, when the birds became hungry. Feeding was also better for catching wigeon. At inland sites, however, dogging was the traditional method of catching.

Nacton (Orwell Park) Decoy cottage was built, before the decoy, for a miller and woodman. (D. Revett/WWT)

Decoys in Britain

Daniel Defoe, writing on his tour of Great Britain in the early eighteenth century, said of the Lincolnshire fens: 'Here are also an infinite number of wild fowl…and for the taking of [them], here are a great number of decoys or duckoys, call them which you please, from all which the vast number of fowls they take are sent up to London. The quantity indeed is incredible…'. Defoe goes on to give a lengthy and admiring, though not necessarily wholly accurate, account of the working of decoys.

In all, at least forty decoys were scattered throughout Lincolnshire. The most famous was in the north, on the edge of Scunthorpe. Ashby Decoy consisted of four pipes on a pond of 2 acres (0.8 ha) in a silver birch wood of 10 acres (4 ha). Payne-Gallwey described it as the most successful in England, with an average catch of nearly 3000 ducks per season, and a record of 6357 in 1834–5. Between 1833 and 1868 nearly 100,000 ducks were caught, including 48,664 mallard, 44,568 teal, 2019 wigeon, 285 shoveler, 278 pintail and 22 gadwall. The re-dug pond now provides irrigation water for a golf course.

There was a cluster of decoys just west of Lincoln, at South Carlton, Burton and Skellingthorpe. It was said that 'certain epicures in London claimed to be able to tell by the flavour of the birds whether they were caught at Burton or at Skellingthorpe'. Skellingthorpe Decoy was constructed towards the end of the seventeenth century and was worked until 1840. A lease dated 1693

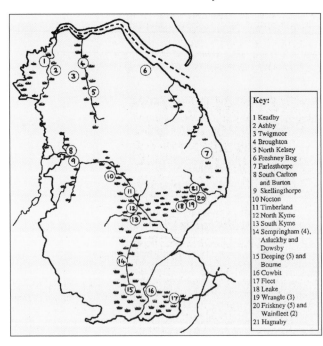

Key:

1 Keadby
2 Ashby
3 Twigmoor
4 Broughton
5 North Kelsey
6 Freshney Bog
7 Farlesthorpe
8 South Carlton
   and Burton
9 Skellingthorpe
10 Nocton
11 Timberland
12 North Kyme
13 South Kyme
14 Sempringham (4),
   Aslackby and
   Dowsby
15 Deeping (5) and
   Bourne
16 Cowbit
17 Fleet
18 Leake
19 Wrangle (3)
20 Friskney (5) and
   Wainfleet (2)
21 Hagnaby

The distribution of decoys in Lincolnshire, closely related to that of the former wetland areas. (After Lorand and Atkin, 1989)

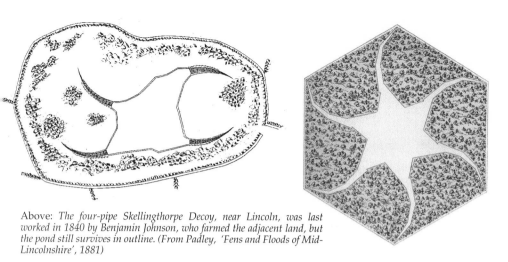

Above: *The four-pipe Skellingthorpe Decoy, near Lincoln, was last worked in 1840 by Benjamin Johnson, who farmed the adjacent land, but the pond still survives in outline. (From Padley, 'Fens and Floods of Mid-Lincolnshire', 1881)*

Right: *A plan of a six-pipe decoy, such as that at Friskney, Lincolnshire.*

granted Humphrey Wilkinson the working of the decoy for a period of twenty-one years, 'paying yearly and every year during the said term yearly rent of sixteen pounds and ten shillings'. At the end of this period he was to 'reasonably and quietly leave, surrender and yield upp [the decoy] so well and sufficiently repaired...together with twenty drakes and fourscore tame ducks'.

The southern Lincolnshire fens probably had a greater concentration of decoys than any other part of England – around thirty, with clusters at Sempringham, Deeping, Wrangle and Friskney. Between them, these decoys were catching huge numbers of ducks. Records for the decoy at Dowsby indicate 13,180 ducks were taken between October 1765 and April 1766 and sold for seven shillings a dozen.

Dersingham Decoy, Norfolk. As with several relict decoys, the former structure is hinted at by rusting hoops over an overgrown pipe.

17

Above left: *At Nacton (Orwell Park), Suffolk, each pipe is overlooked by a rustic observation hut. The decoy's situation, in a small valley, is unusual and reflects its origins as a mill pond.*

Above right: *View of a pipe at Nacton (Orwell Park), looking down from an observation hut.*

Nacton (Orwell Park) Decoy has sunken paths allowing hidden access between the pipes.

Norfolk is well supplied with lakes, in the Broads and elsewhere, which could be converted into duck decoys by the addition of pipes around the edge. Mickle Mere, near East Wretham, was surrounded by ten pipes, built in the 1830s. Most spectacularly, Fritton Lake (partly in Suffolk) had pipes added on three sides by different owners, with at least twenty-one (possibly twenty-three) pipes in place altogether; it was known as Fritton Decoy even in 1783.

At one of the decoys at Fritton it was said that prior to 1848 two hundred ducks were caught daily 'for weeks on end', and three times that number would be taken in a single day on a regular basis. At another, a total of 13,421 birds were caught between 1862 and 1877, roughly 1000 per season. Unusually, one of the Fritton decoys, owned at the end of the nineteenth century by Colonel Leathes and worked by 'old John Fisk', was operated at night: by feeding the ducks early in the season (on dross barley, Indian corn and acorns) and not disturbing them early on, they could be dissuaded from flighting out at dusk and could be taken after dark. Norfolk had smaller decoy ponds as well; Dersingham Decoy, built in 1818 and restored on several occasions, is still visible and managed for amenity.

In 1886, when Payne-Gallwey was writing, Suffolk still had more *working* decoys than any other county – eight, grouped around Nacton, Iken and Fritton – including small ones specifically for teal. The great majority of Suffolk decoys were on or close to the coast, though one well inland at Lakenheath was 'probably the most successful one of its day, owing to its wild locality and surrounding fens'. In the early nineteenth century this decoy was said (perhaps optimistically) to send up to a ton of ducks twice a week to London.

Essex was second only to Lincolnshire in its numbers of decoys – at least thirty, again many of them near the coast. Some of these – at

This four-pipe decoy on Old Hall Marshes, Essex, was a specialist 'teal pond'.

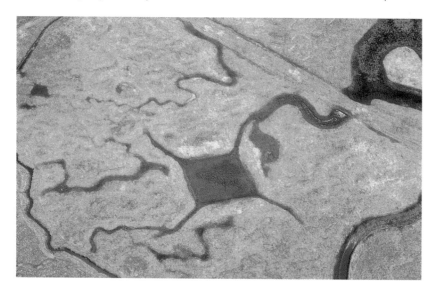

Pennyhole Fleet Decoy, Essex, on Old Hall Marshes, an unusually shaped eight-pipe structure, built in the late eighteenth or early nineteenth century, probably making use of a former saltmarsh creek.

Lion Point and Mersea Island – were specialist 'pochard ponds', at which these diving ducks were caught not in pipes but with nets attached to long poles. Whilst one man put the birds up, a second would release the weighted poles, which sprang upright. The pochard hit the net and fell into pockets at the bottom. Elsewhere, wigeon were the main quarry – Steeple Decoy caught 6286 in 1714–15 amongst a record annual total of 7345 ducks.

There were surprisingly few decoys in the Cambridgeshire fens, though the famous Borough Fen Decoy sent many ducks to market in London. At Chatteris, Payne-Gallwey noted that an old parish map showed 'Site of Decoy erected by Colonel Valentine Warton

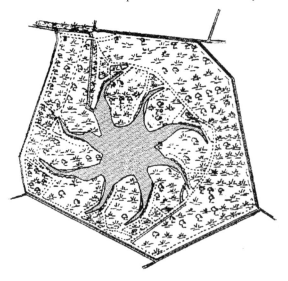

Borough Fen Decoy, near Peterborough, is an example of an eight-pipe decoy, the pipes covering all possible wind directions.

Many decoys had a cottage built close by for the decoyman. This is the decoy house at Boarstall, Buckinghamshire.

destroyed by the populace at the Restoration'. Boarstall Decoy in Buckinghamshire was constructed between 1691 and 1697. Aldwincle, Northamptonshire, had a very late decoy, built for Lord Lilford in 1885, and used for only a few years.

There were relatively small numbers of decoys across the southern English counties, from Kent to Dorset. Virginia Water, in Surrey, had three pipes added to its north shore. The decoy at Pyrford, in the same county, was originally owned by Sir John Wooley, Latin Secretary to Elizabeth I, and thus must have been of an early date. Firle Park, Sussex, had a decoy with a single pipe on a 4 acre (1.6 ha) pond.

In Dorset, the Swannery at Abbotsbury, at the west end of the Fleet, had a famous decoy. Defoe visited Abbotsbury, and also the newly constructed decoy at Morden, where he enjoyed 'a small adventure' – the accidental capture, in a trap set for vermin near the decoy keeper's house, of a large eagle (probably a white-tailed

Abbotsbury, Dorset, at the head of the Fleet, was originally a four-pipe pond. The remains of two pipes directly on to the Fleet can also be seen. (Crown Copyright/MOD)

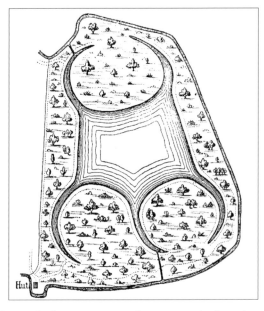

Morden Decoy in Dorset, an unusual design for a five-pipe decoy. The remains of the decoy now form a feature of the Morden Bog National Nature Reserve.

Hut

eagle). Morden Decoy, built to an unusual, asymmetric five-pipe design, was set in a marshy valley surrounded by heathland and was worked until 1856.

The importance of extensive wetland habitat in siting decoys is shown once again by the concentration of decoys in the Somerset Levels, the greatest number outside eastern England. Five were still working in Payne-Gallwey's time, including a group of three small four-pipe decoys on King's Sedgemoor, south-west of Glastonbury. These had been made in 1825 by Joseph Everdell, who was still working in 1886 in his eighties, hooking birds out of the tunnel net with the steel hook that replaced a hand lost in a shooting accident. Ironically, these ponds remained in use for duck-shooting at least until the 1970s.

The decoys of Somerset are well documented. That at Nyland has four leases surviving, the earliest from 1678, and various details of the structure are known – pipe rods, for example, were replaced every seven years, being obtained from Asham Wood near Frome, with nets and twine coming from Wells and tar from Bristol. Westbury (or Stoke) Decoy is a large and complex early structure (probably two decoys), in existence before 1635. In 1676 five tenants constructed a decoy on Aller Moor; the lord of the manor gave construction materials, and in return the tenants were to stock the decoy and give up a quarter of the birds caught. This site is still in good condition. The decoy at Compton Dundon was built in 1695 at a cost of £139 9s 2¹/₂d; by 1720 it was making a yearly profit of £35, and in 1769 it was let by the Earl of Ilchester to John Nitch for seven years at a yearly rent of £30. There was a large ten-pipe decoy at Porlock, near Exmoor (ignored by Payne-Gallwey, who missed several sites in the West Country).

Above: *Crab-shaped or 'skate's-egg' decoys were constructed on the Berkeley estate, Gloucestershire, and elsewhere. This is the Berkeley New Decoy. (Hugh Boyd/WWT)*

Right: *Payne-Gallwey's plan for a crab-shaped decoy, such as those built in Gloucestershire and Monmouthshire.*

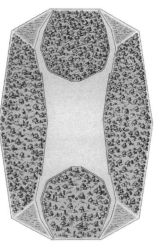

In Gloucestershire, two decoys were constructed east of Purton for the Berkeley estate, each of one acre (0.4 ha) and four pipes. The New Decoy was built in 1843 to replace the Old Decoy when the latter suffered disturbance from the construction of the Gloucester & Sharpness Canal nearby, and both later suffered from shooting locally. In the Midlands, there are examples both of specially constructed decoys (Coombe Abbey and Stoneleigh, Warwickshire) and of pipes being added to ornamental lakes (Packington Hall, Warwickshire; Sundorne Castle, Shropshire).

Berkeley New Decoy, Slimbridge, Gloucestershire. Only about two hundred birds a year are now caught here, for demonstration purposes; greater numbers of ducks are taken in a large swan trap.

In the East Midlands, there was a preference for a different form of decoy – the cage-trap type. The earliest example was constructed at Haughton in Nottinghamshire; it was copied elsewhere in that county and reached its greatest refinement at Hardwick Hall, Derbyshire, where the cage trap was built on a small island in the river Doe Lea. The cage (constructed of hoops and netting, like a pipe) had two compartments, each with a sliding trap door. The doors were worked by wires running back to two windlasses set in a stone 'sight-house'. The trap doors were left in the raised position whilst wild birds were enticed by tame ducks and by feeding; the doors were then carefully lowered, and the trapped ducks removed after flighting time. These cage traps were never as successful as the great pipe decoys – Haughton captured only 300–400 birds annually – but would have supplied local needs.

There were at least fourteen decoys in Yorkshire, with a concentration in the south-east in the extensive marshes of the Humberhead Levels. Doncaster Decoy is of special interest as a municipal, rather than

The stone sight-house at Hardwick Hall, Derbyshire, restored by the National Trust. From here, copper wires operated the gate of a cage decoy.

private, enterprise. In 1657 Doncaster Corporation spent £160 on building a 6 acre (2.4 ha) six-pipe decoy in Balby Carr, the profits from which were to be distributed to the poor of the town. Over the subsequent years the decoy was leased out to a series of different operators (yearly rent in 1696 was set at £18), being finally abandoned around 1778, when the surrounding land had been

Meaux Decoy, east of Beverley, East Yorkshire, an asymmetric four-pipe structure. It is typical of former decoys that are recognisable only as earthworks.

24

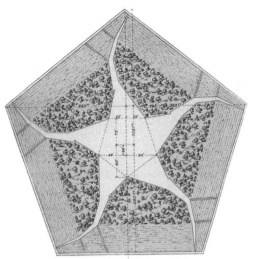

Above: *A plan from Payne-Gallwey's book, indicating the layout of a typical five-pipe decoy, as built at Hale, now in Cheshire.*

Left: *Payne-Gallwey's decoy at Thirkleby Park, North Yorkshire, is now a fishing lake in a caravan park. It retains a plaque indicating its date of construction – 1885.*

drained and converted to agriculture. Railway sidings later obliterated the site; it now lies just outside the Potteric Carr nature reserve, near an area named Decoy Marsh in remembrance.

Of half a dozen decoys on the wetlands of Thorne Moors, some may have been cage, rather than pipe, decoys. These succumbed to agricultural improvement, several being buried by warping (deposition of estuarine silt to improve fertility). By 1886 only two decoys were still operating in Yorkshire, at Hornby Castle and Payne-Gallwey's three-pipe decoy at Thirkleby Park. Another late decoy, at Coatham on the Tees marshes, the most northerly on the east coast, lasted only a very short time – built in 1840, it was affected by the construction of a railway in 1850 and fell out of use.

Decoys elsewhere in northern England were few. Hale Decoy, on the north bank of the Mersey, a five-pipe decoy screened by trees but set within saltmarsh, was surrounded by a moat filled by estuarine water at high tide. This is an ancient decoy – an inscription on stonework has been interpreted as the date 1631. The northernmost decoy in Britain was at Lowther Castle in Cumbria.

Only five duck decoys were apparently ever constructed in Wales. Two of them, at Nash and Wilcrick, lay just east of Newport; each of one acre (0.4 ha) and six pipes, they were owned by Joseph Wilcox of Nash (who also built Berkeley New Decoy). Another was on Llanrhidian Marsh in the Gower peninsula. Little, if anything, remains of these three decoys. Lymore Park, on the edge of Montgomery, is an important landscaped park, one feature of which is a well-preserved decoy with five pipes.

The decoyman at Orielton, Pembrokeshire, Harold Greenslade, releases three ringed wigeon in January 1948. Orielton was the first British decoy where ducks were caught to be ringed.

The best-known of the Welsh decoys is at Orielton, south of Pembroke. Here, four pipes were added to an existing artificial lake in 1868. The Orielton Decoy Book records catches from 1877 to 1912, with a peak of 2521 ducks caught in the winter of 1890–1. The decoy fell into disuse during the First World War but was restored in 1934 to catch birds to be ringed rather than eaten, and this continued until 1950. The naturalist Ronald Lockley wrote of this period, describing dogging with a corgi as a piper and smoking peat on a shovel to disguise the scent. He complained that otters would sometimes catch ducks in the pipe before the decoyman! The decoy fell into disrepair after 1950, though the pipes are still discernible.

Orielton is one of few decoys with comprehensive records of birds caught. Where records are available, the majority show a similar pattern: the most frequent ducks caught by far are mallard and teal, the most numerous species in winter. Other species – pintail, wigeon, shoveler – are much less frequent. Gadwall were also rare; the recent increase in numbers of this species is believed to have started with a pair trapped at Dersingham Decoy around 1850, then wing-clipped and

Right: *A pair of mallard – the mallard is the most numerous duck in Britain and generally the commonest duck caught in decoys. (Jonathan Leach/WWT)*

Below right: *Teal, the smallest British duck, and a species caught almost as frequently as mallard in decoys. Small specialist 'teal ponds' were sometimes constructed, as at Nacton. (Keith Stone/WWT)*

Below: *A male gadwall – a species caught infrequently in decoys, but which has been increasing in numbers. (Philippa Scott/WWT)*

Pochard, as diving ducks, were difficult to catch in traditional decoys. East coast counties had specialist pochard ponds with high nets to catch the ducks as they took off. (Jonathan Leach/WWT)

kept at Narford Lake in Breckland, where they bred, giving rise to a substantial East Anglian population.

These species are all dabbling ducks, feeding mainly on the surface of the water and hence easily enticed by fed grain. Diving ducks – pochard and tufted duck – were more rarely caught; even if drawn into the net, they tended to dive to escape, evading the decoyman and swimming back underwater to the open pond. However, certain decoys in Essex and Suffolk were built specifically as 'dunbird' (pochard) ponds, with tall nets. In London, dunbirds were known as 'esteemed excellent eating'.

Several decoys in East Anglia were catching over 5000 ducks a year. Borough Fen's best season was 1804–5, with 5408 ducks caught. The ten decoys around Wainfleet caught 31,200 birds in one year around 1768. Late on in the age of decoys, Nacton averaged 3903 birds a year between 1919 and 1969, and Abbotsbury had its best catch, 1476, in 1926. Even in as unlikely a place for ducks as the

	Ducks.	Teal.	Widgeon.	Shoveller.	Pintail.	Gadwall.	Total.
1833–34	1884	1232	102	...	9	...	3227
1834–35	4287	1860	140	16	54	...	6357
1835–36	959	788	38	16	7	...	1808
1836–37	768	326	24	14	...	...	1132
1837–38	1511	509	47	11	4	...	2082
1838–39	758	791	21	2	4	...	1576
1839–40	2014	2002	24	21	74	...	4205
1840–41	2584	993	126	13	8	...	3724
1841–42	1666	908	28	5	6	...	2613
1842–43	1094	2077	49	6	2	...	3228
1843–44	1004	1036	88	3	3	...	2135
1844–45	1298	1181	65	1	2	1	2547
1845–46	1022	1321	39	3	5	1	2390
1846–47	1428	905	43	5	4	1	2486
1847–48	1212	883	36	...	1	1	2133
1848–49	1740	1971	53	9	5	...	3778
1849–50	1145	956	27	...	2	1	2131
1850–51	380	853	34	...	3	...	1270
1851–52	632	1003	72	1	2	1	1711
1852–53	2682	3279	67	2	26	3	6059
1853–54	2425	1605	75	1	3	2	4111
1854–55	1298	1221	89	3	2	3	2616
1855–56	1004	781	33	4	4	...	1836
1856–57	763	771	27	11	1	2	1575
1857–58	634	1566	110	24	11	3	2348
1858–59	715	1208	82	4	4	...	2023
1859–60	734	1204	83	7	1	...	2029
1860–61	1121	2365	23	34	3	1	3747
1861–62	1605	1145	54	11	6	1	2822
1862–63	843	1481	25	14	1	...	2464
1863–64	2326	1842	82	20	6	1	4277
1864–65	1663	1205	85	5	1	...	2959
1865–66	282	637	17	...	...	...	936
1866–67	1891	1502	66	4	12	...	3475
1867–68	1292	1161	75	15	2	...	2545

A record of wildfowl taken at Ashby Decoy, Lincolnshire. Only mallard were seen as 'full ducks', other species being counted as 'half ducks'.

Above left: *Gregory Gill, the Fleet swanherd who was also decoyman at Abbotsbury, Dorset, from 1879 to 1922. Gill's family worked at Abbotsbury over several generations.*

Above right: *Tom Baker, decoyman at Nacton (Orwell Park), Suffolk, with a catch in the decoy storehouse, when the decoy was still in commercial use.*

Dorset heaths, Morden Decoy was averaging around 400 ducks per season between 1774 and 1795. This indicates not only the huge numbers of birds available to be caught in these times, but also the value to the local economy.

Prices paid for decoy-caught birds are known in some instances. Records from Abbotsbury show that in 1662 mallards sold for a shilling and teal for 5d. By 1793 mallards were 2s to 3s and teal 1s 6d to 2s; at this time the Abbotsbury decoyman was paying 12s for 2 bushels of hempseed as bait. In 1926 prices were not much greater – 4s 6d for mallard and 1s 8d for teal. Figures for Borough Fen birds in the mid nineteenth century show the comparative value of the species caught – mallard 1s 2d to 1s 5d, pintail 1s, wigeon and shoveler 8d, teal $6^{1}/_{2}$d. Prices fluctuated, increasing with the blockades of the Napoleonic wars, and dropping in the late nineteenth century as ducks imported from the numerous Dutch decoys flooded the market.

The earliest British decoys were built by Dutch decoymen, but two English families were greatly involved in spreading the idea of decoys around the country. One was the Skeltons of Friskney, Lincolnshire; 'Old George' Skelton, born in 1760, constructed the six-pipe Friskney Decoy in the late eighteenth century, then moved in 1807 to build Winterton and other decoys in Norfolk, where he died in 1840. George's sons and other members of the family were involved with decoys all over England, including Coombe Abbey, Warwickshire,

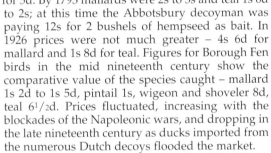

'Old George' Skelton, described as 'short of stature, web-footed like a duck, very strongly built, particularly kind in disposition, perfectly indifferent to cold and hardship'.

Above: *Daniel White was the decoyman at Boarstall Decoy, Buckinghamshire, from 1869. The Aubrey and Aubrey-Fletcher families ran the decoy for 250 years, until the Second World War.*

Above: *Billy Williams, decoyman at Borough Fen from 1929 to 1958, was the last of the Williams family to work there. Here he is ringing a teal, watched by his piper dog, Amber.*

made by William Skelton in 1845, and Aldwincle, Northamptonshire, built by Thomas Gilbert Skelton in 1885.

The Williams family of Borough Fen in Cambridgeshire was the other great decoy dynasty. The first Williams was recorded working there in 1670, after which a continuous line of Williams decoymen ran the site until the death of Billy Williams in 1958. Various members of the family were also involved with decoys in Lincolnshire and elsewhere: John Williams (1779–1855) built four pipes on to the ornamental lake at Packington Hall, Warwickshire, whilst John Bradley Williams (1820–99) designed a pipe for Orielton and worked on the abortive Scottish decoy at Findhorn. Earlier, Andrew Williams had left Borough Fen to work the decoy at Aston Hall, Shropshire; upon his death, an epitaph composed for him described the strange life of a decoyman.

Below left: *Jim Worgan, the decoyman at Boarstall in 2001, sends his former piper, Don, a Kooikerhondje, through the decoy.*

Below right: *Epitaph for Andrew Williams, who was born in 1693 and died on 18th April 1776, having served as decoyman under the Aston family for sixty years at Aston Hall, Shropshire, by the river Perry.*

" Here lies the Decoyman who lived like an otter,

Dividing his time betwixt land and water ;

His hide he oft soaked in the waters of Perry,

Whilst Aston old beer his spirits kept cheery.

Amphibious his life, Death was puzzled to say

How to dust to reduce such well-moistened clay.

So Death turned Decoyman, and 'coyed him to land,

Where he fixed his abode till quite dried to the hand.

He then found him fitting for crumbling to dust ;

And here he lies mouldering as you and I must."

Decline of the decoys

By the mid nineteenth century the number of working decoys had declined drastically as unproductive ones were abandoned. This was mainly due to the widespread drainage of wetlands brought about by the various Drainage Acts: there was no longer the extent of habitat to attract wintering birds from the Continent, and the numbers of British breeding ducks had similarly fallen. When the Lincolnshire fenland was drained the number of highly productive decoys around Wainfleet fell from ten to three even by 1829.

Disturbance also played a part. The increasing availability and efficiency of firearms, especially with the introduction of rapid breech loading, meant that shooting was competing with and directly affecting decoys. The two decoys at Berkeley, Gloucestershire, were said to be ruined by the Ground Game Act of 1880, constant shooting scaring the wildfowl away. Benacre Broad

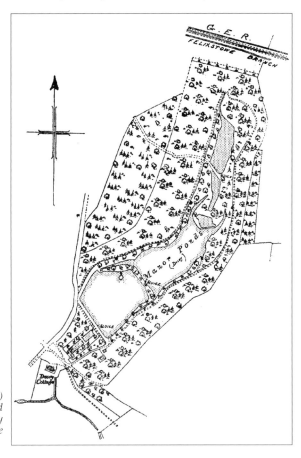

The ponds at Nacton (Orwell Park) Decoy, Suffolk, originally provided power for a watermill and were only later converted to two decoys (the smaller one for teal).

Above left: *Ringing a mallard with an individually numbered metal leg ring. The bird-ringing scheme in the United Kingdom is organised by the British Trust for Ornithology. (L. Dwyer/WWT)*

Above right: *The decoyman at Slimbridge, Gloucestershire, Dave Paynter, ringing a mallard caught in Berkeley New Decoy.*

Right: *Releasing a ringed mallard at Slimbridge.*

Decoy, Suffolk, was constructed in 1880 but the local shooting was let soon after and it was never used.

Developments near decoys also brought about a fall in numbers. Fleet Decoy in Lincolnshire (once owned by Joseph Banks) was destroyed by the cutting of the South Holland Drain in 1793. Joseph Wilcox, the owner of the two decoys near Newport, was paid £500 compensation when the Great Western Railway was constructed within half a mile (800 metres) of them. Coatham Decoy, on Teesside, was also affected by a railway and closed following the construction of nearby ironworks.

By the time of his survey in 1918, Joseph Whitaker was able to report that only twenty-one decoys were still in use. The decline

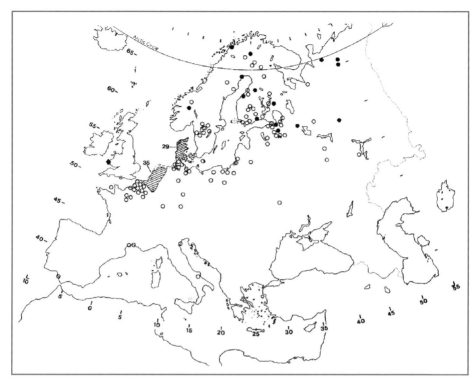

continued into the twentieth century – by 1936 only eleven remained working. The last decoy in commercial use was Nacton (Orwell Park) in Suffolk. This operated (very successfully, catching 9303 birds in 1925–6) from 1830 to 1968, when the Wildfowl Trust took on a lease to catch birds for ringing, which continued until 1982.

This change from catching birds for food to ringing and releasing them had taken place in all the remaining working decoys by the second half of the twentieth century. The first decoy to go this way was Orielton; from refurbishment in 1934 until 1950 11,000 ducks were ringed, providing some of the earliest insights into wildfowl migration. Ringing followed at Nacton and the other extant decoys, peaking at over 8000 birds ringed at six decoys in 1967. Recoveries of these ringed birds (Nacton pintails in Russia, Orielton teal across Scandinavia, a Borough Fen wigeon at Tomsk in Siberia and mallard in Alberta, Canada) demonstrate the widespread provenance of the ducks that had fed the British over the centuries.

Decoys today

There remain just four working decoys in Britain out of the two hundred or so which formerly existed. The best-preserved is that at Borough Fen, north of Peterborough. The 2¹/₂ acre (1 ha) pond is surrounded by eight pipes, each one in working order, set in 14¹/₂ acres (6 ha) of woodland. For three centuries the Williams family worked the decoy, sending birds to Leadenhall Market in London – originally by stage down the Great North Road, later by railway from the local station at Deeping St James. Latterly, the Wildfowl and Wetlands Trust has funded the site for ringing purposes. The decoy is a Scheduled Ancient Monument.

The other decoy operated by the Wildfowl and Wetlands Trust is at its headquarters at Slimbridge, Gloucestershire. This is Berkeley New Decoy, constructed in 1843, a four-pipe structure, the two pipes

Left: *Borough Fen, Cambridgeshire, an eight-pipe decoy with all the pipes in working order. Not only of historic importance, as an Ancient Monument, it is also an island of wildlife habitat in a sea of arable land.*

Below: *The decoyman's hut at Slimbridge, Gloucestershire, now houses a display explaining the working of a decoy to the site's thousands of visitors.*

on either side curving towards each other. It provided ducks for the owners of Berkeley Castle. The Trust took it over when it established its Slimbridge reserve in 1946, since when many thousands of birds have been ringed here. Exhibitions have been set up in a hide overlooking the decoy and in the old decoyman's hut, and demonstrations are given.

The early history of Boarstall Decoy in Buckinghamshire is unclear, the oldest known record being on a map of 1697. Originally a six-pipe decoy, it provided ducks for the Aubreys and Aubrey-Fletchers of Boarstall House for nearly 250 years, with any surplus sold in local markets and London. Average catches in the late nineteenth century were 800 per year, but decoying ceased during the Second World War. Catching resumed in 1963 and continued until 1974 under the direction of the Wildfowlers Association of Great Britain and Ireland, to provide ducks for breeding stock. In 1980 the decoy was purchased by the National Trust, following which two pipes were fully restored. The decoy is still worked with a dog by the decoyman for ringing, and the National Trust has a visitor centre on the site.

The Swannery at Abbotsbury, Dorset, which had provided fresh meat to the Benedictine monastery from 1393 until the Dissolution, and then to the Strangways family, was supplemented from about 1655 by the produce of a four-pipe decoy, and also of two pipes built directly on to the Fleet. Detailed records of catches exist from 1881; in 1912 a Dutch-ringed teal turned up at the decoy. Since 1937 Abbotsbury birds have been ringed rather than killed –

Above centre: *Restoring the 'home pipe' at Boarstall Decoy, Buckinghamshire, in 1986 – setting up new reed screens.*

Above: *Inside the National Trust's visitor centre at Boarstall Decoy, showing the mural and display on decoys.*

Above left: *Hale Decoy, Cheshire, lies beneath the flight path into Liverpool Airport. It was used to catch ducks for ringing but is no longer operated.*

Above right: *Abbotsbury Decoy, Dorset, constructed in 1655, is probably the oldest decoy still in use in Britain.*

Centre right: *The decoyman's house at Abbotsbury, destroyed by a tidal wave in 1824, was rebuilt and now serves as an information centre.*

Bottom right: *At Abbotsbury one of the visitor features is a model decoy pipe for children to crawl through.*

mostly teal, with occasional birds other than wildfowl, such as water rail, bittern and snipe. Three pipes remain working, and the whole site is a significant tourist attraction.

Until the late 1990s Hale Decoy near the Mersey was managed by Cheshire Wildlife Trust. One of the five pipes was completely restored and used for ringing. However, the Trust's tenancy has now ended, and the decoy appears no longer to be active. Nacton (Orwell Park), Suffolk, also remains in working order, with four pipes restored, but is not regularly operated.

Apart from the working decoys, the remains of a number of former decoys are given protection in some way. Thirty decoys have been scheduled as Ancient Monuments by English Heritage, half of them in Somerset. Only two are scheduled in Lincolnshire (Skellingthorpe and Aslackby), and none in Norfolk or Suffolk – perhaps

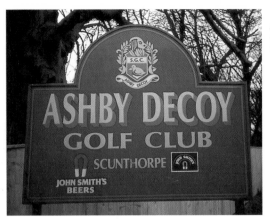

Ashby Decoy, near Scunthorpe, Lincolnshire, now provides irrigation water for a golf club, which is named after the feature.

demonstrating better survival in the less intensively farmed West Country.

Several decoys that served country houses still remain on estates which are now more accessible to the public. The park at the National Trust's Hardwick Hall in Derbyshire includes the site of a cage-trap decoy (now wet woodland), and one of the stone sight-houses has been restored. Similarly, Thompson's Wood at Wollaton Park, Nottingham, was formerly a decoy. At Coombe Country Park, Coventry, the decoy, built in 1880 to supply the Coombe Abbey estate, now provides a pond-dipping area. Thirkleby Decoy, North Yorkshire, is now a fishing lake in a caravan park.

Quite apart from their historical value, relict decoys can retain significant wildlife interest, such that they rate protection as Sites of Special Scientific Interest (SSSIs). In some instances, the decoys fall within larger SSSIs – Berkeley and Hale on the Severn and Mersey estuaries respectively, and Acle in the Broads. At least two National Nature Reserves, Morden Bog and Bure Marshes, encompass decoys.

The former Aldwincle Decoy, Northamptonshire, is now a wood that supports a large heronry within Titchmarsh Local Nature Reserve. The Royal Society for the Protection of Birds filmed the documentary 'Big Bill the Heron' here in 1972.

Elsewhere, the decoy itself, with its surrounding woodland, provides the interest. Titchmarsh Duck Decoy SSSI comprises the three-pipe pond and mixed woodland of Aldwincle Decoy; one of the largest heronries in Northamptonshire, it forms part of Titchmarsh Local Nature Reserve. Friskney Decoy Wood is a nature reserve of the Lincolnshire Wildlife Trust. The decoy, the first one associated with the Skelton family, went out of use in 1878, but it is still possible to trace the course of the pipes, and the re-dug pond provides a home for dragonflies.

Above: Ranworth Broad, part of the Bure Marshes National Nature Reserve in Norfolk, was formerly the site of a ten-pipe decoy taking about a thousand birds a season.

The Decoy Inn, near Borough Fen, Cambridgeshire. 'Decoy' often crops up in place names, such as Decoy Farm and Decoy House, though it may indicate a shooting pond rather than a trap.

The pond at Stoneleigh Decoy, Warwickshire, as at many former decoys, has developed into wet woodland – a key biodiversity habitat.

Confusingly, the name 'decoy' has been transferred to flight ponds where ducks were attracted to be shot rather than trapped. Thus, many 'decoy ponds' named on maps never had any pipe or cage structure associated with them, and this sometimes makes it difficult to identify former decoy sites. Nevertheless, there remains a surprisingly large number of relict decoys listed in county Sites and Monuments Records. Some of these were not identified by Payne-Gallwey – at Stoneleigh, Warwickshire, the Royal Agricultural Society of England estate includes a four-pipe, seventeenth-century decoy which does not appear in *The Book of Duck Decoys*.

In south Devon, a decoy pond is being restored by the naturalist Tony Soper. At Coombe, Warwickshire, and Fritton, Suffolk, one pipe of each decoy is to be restored. With an increasing interest in the historic environment, and funding available through schemes such as Countryside Stewardship, it may be that more of these fascinating features could be brought back to something near their original form.

The former Stoneleigh Decoy, Warwickshire, now serves as one point on the Royal Agricultural Society of England's farm trail.

Further reading

Cook, Tony, and Pilcher, R.E.M. *The History of Borough Fen Decoy.* Providence Press, 1982.

Day, James Wentworth. *A History of the Fens.* Harrap, 1954.

Defoe, Daniel. *A Tour through the Whole Island of Great Britain, 1724–5.* Everyman's Library, 1962 (originally published in 1727).

Fair, John, and Moxom, Don. *Abbotsbury and the Swannery.* Dovecote Press, 1993.

Fowler, Diana, and Eckly, Simon. *The Wildfowl and Wetlands Trust.* The Archive Photograph Series. Chalford Publishing Company, 1996.

Kear, Janet. *Man and Wildfowl.* Poyser, 1990.

Limbert, Martin. *The Natural Harvest of Thorne Moors.* Thorne and Hatfield Papers, volume 5. Thorne and Hatfield Moors Conservation Forum, 1998.

Lockley, Ronald. *Orielton: The Human and Natural History of a Welsh Manor.* André Deutsch, 1977.

Lorand, Stephen, and Atkin, Keith. *The Birds of Lincolnshire and South Humberside.* Leading Edge Press & Publishing, 1989.

Payne-Gallwey, Ralph. *The Book of Duck Decoys, Their Construction, Management and History.* 1886.

Prendergast, E.D.V. *Dorset Decoys: Abbotsbury and Morden.* Dorset Natural History and Archaeological Society, 1987.

Rackham, Oliver. *The History of the Countryside.* Dent, 1986.

Roach, Alistair. *Boarstall Duck Decoy.* National Trust, 1991.

Stott, Tim, and Mitchell, Carl. 'Orielton Duck Decoy: The Story of Its Decline'. *Field Studies* 7, pages 759–69, 1991.

Whitaker, Joseph. *British Duck Decoys of Today, 1918.* 1918.

Websites

www.decoymans.freeserve.co.uk (includes the text of Payne-Gallwey, 1886, and Whitaker, 1918)

www.eng-h.gov.uk/mpp/mcd/sub/decoy.htm (information about decoys from English Heritage's Monuments Protection Programme)

Ducks sit on the pond at Nacton (Orwell Park) Decoy, Suffolk. (C. P. Rose/WWT)

Places to visit

In order to avoid disappointment, intending visitors are advised to telephone to find out the opening times before making a special journey.

Abbotsbury Swannery, New Barn Road, Abbotsbury, Dorset DT3 4JG. Telephone: 01305 871684. Working decoy, decoyman's hut with exhibition, model pipe for children.

Boarstall Duck Decoy, Boarstall, near Aylesbury, Buckinghamshire HP18 9UX (National Trust). Telephone: 01844 237488. Working decoy, exhibition hall, nature trail.

Borough Fen Decoy, near Peterborough, Cambridgeshire. Access on open days only; details from Peakirk Wildfowl World, Deeping Road, Peakirk PE6 7NP. Telephone: 01733 252271. Working decoy.

Bure Marshes National Nature Reserve, Norfolk. Details from Norfolk Wildlife Trust, Broadland Conservation Centre, Ranworth, Norfolk. Telephone: 01603 270479. Website: www.wildlifetrust.org.uk/norfolk Disused decoy on nature trail; display in visitor centre.

Coombe Country Park, Brinklow Road, Binley, near Coventry CV3 2AB. Telephone: 02476 453270. Decoy pond used for pond-dipping.

Decoy Spinney, Stoneleigh, Warwickshire. Access by prior agreement with Royal Agricultural Society of England, National Agricultural Centre, Stoneleigh. Telephone: 02476 696969. Disused decoy on farm trail.

Denaby Ings, near Doncaster. Details from Yorkshire Wildlife Trust, 10 Toft Green, York YO1 1JT. Telephone: 01904 659570. Disused decoy in nature reserve.

Friskney Decoy Wood, Friskney, Lincolnshire. Details from Lincolnshire Wildlife Trust, Banovallum House, Manor House Street, Horncastle, Lincolnshire LN9 5HF. Telephone: 01507 526667. Website: www.lincstrust.co.uk Disused decoy in nature reserve.

Fritton Lake Countryworld, near Great Yarmouth, Norfolk. Telephone: 01493 488208. Restored pipe on decoy lake.

Hardwick Hall, Doe Lea, Chesterfield, Derbyshire S44 5QJ (National Trust). Telephone: 01246 850430. Site of cage-trap decoy, stone decoy hide.

Morden Bog National Nature Reserve, near Wareham, Dorset. (Permit holders only.) Details from English Nature, Slepe Farm, Arne, Wareham, Dorset BH20 5BN. Telephone: 01929 557450. Disused decoy.

Nacton (Orwell Park) Decoy, Suffolk. Open to educational groups by arrangement. Contact the Decoyman, John Norris, Decoy House, Nacton, Ipswich, Suffolk IP10 0HP. Telephone: 01473 659302. Website: www.homeusers.prestel.co.uk/decoymans/decoy.htm Restored decoy.

Slimbridge Wildfowl and Wetlands Trust, Slimbridge, Gloucestershire GL2 7BT. Telephone: 01453 891900. Website: www.wwt.org.uk Working decoy, decoyman's hut with exhibition, demonstrations.

Titchmarsh Local Nature Reserve, near Thrapston, Northamptonshire. Details from the Wildlife Trust for Northamptonshire, Lings House, Billing Lings, Northampton NN3 8BE. Telephone: 01604 405285. Website: www.wildlifetrust.org.uk/bcnp Disused decoy with heronry.

Wollaton Hall Natural History Museum, Wollaton Park, Nottingham NG8 2AE. Telephone: 0115 915 3900. Disused decoy on nature trail; park exhibition in visitor centre.